Drawings by Sydney R. Jones of pargeted decoration on the Sun Inn, Saffron Walden, Essex (from 'The Village Homes of England', published 1912).

PARGETING

Tim Buxbaum

Shire Publications

Contents

Cover: *(Right and bottom left) The Ancient House, Clare, Suffolk; (top left) an Arts and Crafts influenced private house on the Suffolk-Essex border.*

ACKNOWLEDGEMENTS
The photographs are all by the author.

British Library Cataloguing in Publication Data: Buxbaum, Tim. Pargeting. – (Shire album; no. 341) 1. Plastering – Great Britain – History 2. Plastering – Technique I. Title 693.6'09 ISBN 0 7478 0414 1

Published in 1999 by Shire Publications Ltd, Cromwell House, Church Street, Princes Risborough, Buckinghamshire HP27 9AA, UK. (Website www.shirebooks.co.uk)
Copyright © 1999 by Tim Buxbaum. First published 1999. Shire Album 341. ISBN 0 7478 0414 1.
Tim Buxbaum is hereby identified as the author of this work in accordance with Section 77 of the Copyright, Designs and Patents Act 1988.

Printed in Great Britain by CIT Printing Services Ltd, Press Buildings, Merlins Bridge, Haverfordwest, Pembrokeshire SA61 1XF.

Introduction

'Some men wyll have thyr wallys plastered, some pergetted and whytelymed, some roughe caste, some pricked, some wrought with playster of Paris.' (William Hormann, *Vulgaria*, 1519)

Pargeting is the ornamentation of plastered and rendered building façades that would otherwise have been left smooth or rough-cast or pebble-dashed. It is surface decoration, only skin-deep, and has been practised in England for over four hundred years. At its simplest it is no more than lines scratched into the wet plaster; at its most complex it encompasses iconography and figurative sculpture. The delicacy and subtlety of the medium and its response to sunlight have enhanced many historic buildings, although numbers have perished from neglect, redevelopment, changing taste and fire. Today pargeting is commonly associated with Essex and rural East Anglia, and with cottages rather than

grand buildings. This reflects the traditional East Anglian preference to finish timber-framed buildings externally in plaster, while in Kent it may have been supplementary to weatherboarding and in Surrey to tile-hanging. Concealing the timber frame became an issue when best-quality green oak began to run short, and this seems to have occurred earlier in East Anglia than elsewhere. Nevertheless, pargeted buildings are documented across England, at least from Canterbury to York. Often these buildings no longer exist: pargeting is inevitably more likely to survive in rural areas than in expanding towns and cities.

Above and left: *Pargeted decoration on the façade of a seventeenth-century property in Hertford, showing both lightly impressed panels of fantail decoration and more substantial floral patterns built up in high relief.*

3

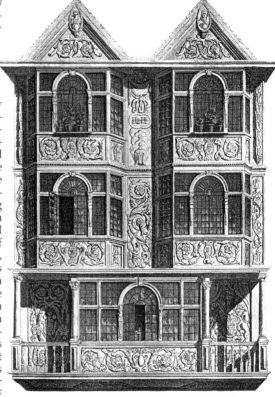

Older pargeting is generally of three sorts: calm, quiet, dateless patterning on rural buildings; extravagant, individualistic displays typically associated with the latter part of the seventeenth century; or 'Olde English' work designed by Victorian architects. No pargeting is known to have survived from before the reign of Elizabeth I (1558–1603): the date panel of 1473 on the Ancient House, Clare, Suffolk, certainly relates to work carried out very much later. Town fires of the seventeenth century seem likely to have destroyed much early pargeting on timber-framed inns, merchants' houses and weaving shops. The Great Fire of London (1666) was particularly significant in so far as it led to the enactment of legislation that required new buildings to have external walls of brick or stone, and these were less likely to have been pargeted.

At its most skilful, pargeting is both art and craft, yet few architectural history books devote much space to it. Regarded neither as a decorative art nor as a useful trade, its development is poorly documented. Produced by an artisan rather than an intellectual or an artist, good pargeting has sensuous, textural qualities and allegorical dimensions, and its success is usually related to rhythm, scale and proportion. More a technique than a style, pargeting has freedom and breadth, encompassing elements of sculpture and folk art. In early times it was a means of expressing personal wealth and social status – an easy way to change completely the appearance of almost any building.

Pargeting is best appreciated in sunlight. As the sun's rays slowly advance, one can watch them illuminate the edges of plaster figures, tendrils and mouldings, which seem to rise up from their shadowed background into counterpoints of changing life, light and shadow. And if the façade is not quite regular, the wall not quite square or plumb, and the surface texture rich, then the drama of light is so much greater. It seems hardly accidental that so much pargeting is orientated to benefit particularly from the long low morning and late afternoon sun.

4

The origins of decorative pargeting

The origins of decorative pargeting are unclear. The historian L. F. Salzman records the use of the term 'pargeting' as early as 1237, when it related to the finishing of internal walls, elaborated in 1423 at Brigstock Park by a 'mason hired to do the daubing, namely, bemfyllynge, herlynge, pargetyng, plastryng and wasshyng (or whytlymyng)'. What inspired builders, owners or the pargeters themselves to broaden their skills into simple though effective patterning is not certain, but it was probably a vernacular response to the great expansion of architectural and artistic knowledge generated by the Renaissance. The rediscovery of the culture of the classical world of Greece and Rome inspired imitation and innovation in art, design and techniques, which spread from Italy throughout Europe.

Two of the most important books on plastering were written by William Millar and G. P. Bankart, published respectively in 1897 and 1908. In his book *The Art of the Plasterer* Bankart distinguished four types of plaster: *stucco duro*, parge, plaster of Paris, and 'modern' fibrous plaster cast in gelatine moulds (superseding earlier moulds of wax or boxwood). *Stucco duro* and parge have the greatest relevance to a study of pargeting, although this is a simplification; the English language does not have a precise vocabulary common both to artisans and historians to distinguish the nuances of the production and application of plasters, stuccos and renders. In this book, for convenience, 'plaster' describes any internal or external wall covering with a sand and lime base, whereas 'render' is reserved for external finishes gauged with cement.

Stucco was known to the Roman writer Vitruvius, who described plaster containing

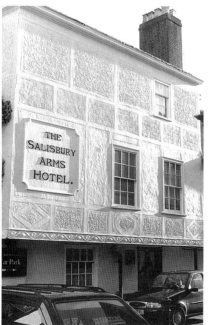

The façade of the Salisbury Arms Hotel, Hertford, is divided up into a series of panels of simply textured decoration. The framework of these panels relates clearly to window openings and floor levels and there is a pargeted vine frieze at the jetting.

5

Pargeting of roundels and impressed patterns on the façade of a building in Clare, Suffolk.

finely sieved marble dust and other carefully selected and matured ingredients, best beaten, chopped and knocked about to achieve malleability and great toughness. Its remarkable qualities may have come from the addition of fig juice, hog's lard, curdled milk, wax or pitch and, to retard the setting or soften the set, sugar, rice, gluten, egg-white and blood. White stucco was used to decorate the buildings of ancient Rome, such as the Baths of Trajan, which, when unearthed, provided the inspiration for Raphael's rhythmic decoration of medallions, cameos and figures in the painted Loggias of the Vatican – a gallery 65 metres (213 feet) long commissioned by Pope Julius II in 1512 from Bramante, continued by and generally credited to Raphael under Pope Leo X. The thirteen arches of these Loggias, so evocative of ancient Roman art, were tremendously influential – for example Catherine II of Russia (reigned 1762-96) commissioned a copy for the Hermitage Palace – and from them Raphael developed elaborate high-relief stucco decoration for the Palazzo Branconio dell'Aquila and the Villa Madama (begun 1516), inspiring others to emulate this form of architectural decoration and even use it for sculpture.

The techniques of the Italian stucco workshops were not ignored in England. Henry VIII employed plasterers with these new skills on the walls of his Nonsuch Palace, built around 1538 in Surrey. Etchings produced before it was demolished show a substantial, fantastic edifice with great octagonal corner towers and façades divided into panels or compartments externally decorated with plaster figures and animals. The upper storey of the inner court was timber-framed and 'richly adorned and set forth and garnished with a variety of pictures and other antick forms of excellent art and workmanship, and of no small cost'. Hentzner, visiting in 1598, wrote: 'one would imagine everything that architecture could perform to have been employed on this work. There are everywhere statues that seem to breathe.' The Duke of Saxe-Weimar elaborated in 1613: 'the labours of Hercules were set forth on the king's side, the queen's side exhibiting all kinds of heathen stories with naked

6

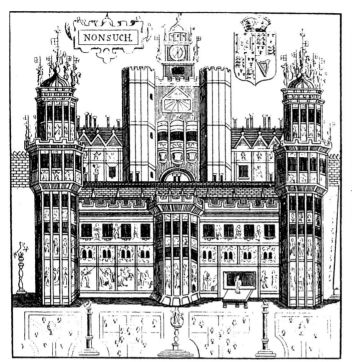

Drawing of Nonsuch Palace, Surrey, based on an old print, showing the building as it may have been around 1620. Plasterwork of the towers and façades (including the courtyard) is divided up into panels pargeted with what appear to be life-sized figures. (Taken from 'London in the Time of the Tudors' by Sir Walter Besant, 1904.)

female figures.' Other visitors mistakenly thought the figures were carved from stone. Nonsuch was pillaged by Cromwell, then given away by Charles II to a mistress, who sold it, and nothing remains; the closest comparison is at Fontainebleau, where stucco executed by Francesco Primaticcio (c.1504-70) was commissioned by Francis I, Henry VIII's great rival. The figurative work at Nonsuch must have been extremely influential and would have received additional publicity in 1666, when, according to the diarist John Evelyn, the building was used by the Exchequer as a refuge from the Plague.

It cannot have been easy to procure suitable marble dust in England for *stucco duro*, and other materials were substituted, including, possibly, rye dough. Italian stucco seems to have been too complex a material to be sustained in widespread use, but the patterning associated with it must have inspired existing pargeters who had been using their coarser, leather-hard, home-grown English product for generations. That was what Bankart described as 'parge', a mixture of sand, lime and hair with a variety of uses, including 'parging' the inside of a chimney flue and under-lining roof tiles, as well as being a plaster finish for walls, to reduce draughts. From such sources developed many of the themes of early interior and exterior plasterwork and render – an enormous subject, of which pargeting is but a small part. Today the word 'pargeting' is used to describe external decoration only.

From the time when Nonsuch was being built, internal plaster friezes were appearing in great houses. They became widespread throughout England and were especially popular on chimney overmantels, depicting processional scenes, groups of figures, animals and monsters, particularly effective when the fire below was lit. Grander examples remain at Cardinal Wolsey's Closet, Hampton Court, Middlesex (c.1525), Loseley Park, Surrey (1568), and Corpus Christi College, Oxford (c.1570). At Hardwick Old Hall, Derbyshire (c.1590), the frieze depicts stags and lilies, and the

7

new Hardwick Hall, completed in 1597, contains a great coloured frieze in the Presence Chamber showing Diana and her nymphs in a forest, disporting themselves amongst lions, elephants and camels. Such friezes were the internal counterpart of the most elaborate external pargeting, as were the spectacular decorative English plaster ceilings being created around 1600. These took motifs from pattern books, from tapestries and embroideries with figurative designs, from armorials, from iconography and from geometrical layouts relating to knot gardens, herbs, mythical beasts and the supernatural. The resulting patterns were triumphantly let loose inside Powis Castle, Powys (1592), Burton Agnes Hall, East Yorkshire (1601–10), Knole, Kent (Cartoon Gallery, 1607), Chastleton House, Oxfordshire (1614), Blickling Hall, Norfolk (1619–20), and Herringstone Manor, Dorset (Great Chamber, c.1620), to name just a few. It is likely that earlier strapwork studded with rosettes and pyramids evolved into freer arabesques with festoons and grotesques, developing further to include allegorical personifications and emblems.

Nineteenth-century writers such as Sir Reginald Blomfield suggested that in the early seventeenth century there were many gabled, jetted houses and riverside palaces in London decorated with pargeting. Blomfield deduced this from his study of old engravings and illustrations, but unfortunately his sources have not been identified. It is tantalising to imagine London full of pargeted buildings, but one should bear in mind that engravers also illustrate other forms of applied decoration. Thus Goldsmith's Row, London, originally built in 1491, was described in 1598 as being faced with the likenesses of woodmen riding on monstrous beasts. This might sound as though it was pargeted, but the decoration was cast in lead, richly painted over and gilded. The house of a wealthy diplomat, Sir Paul Pindar, provides another example. In 1599 he returned to London from Italy and built his house at 169 Bishopsgate. The fashionable bay front was jetted and subdivided into decorated panels. One might have expected these to be pargeted: that is how they look in Thomas Percy's etching made in 1881. But when the house was demolished in 1890 (to make way for Liverpool Street station) the façade was kept; it is now in the gift shop of the Victoria and Albert Museum, and the panels are solid carved oak. Thus there are risks in concluding that an old drawing shows pargeting when it may be illustrating another material, and another layer of confusion is possible when plasterwork is stamped with decorative motifs emulating terracotta facings, for these can bestow the appearance of masonry upon a timber-framed building. Finally, old pargeting is notoriously difficult to date, and even date panels can be deceptive since they may have been reused from earlier works.

The wide variety of pargeted designs that appeared in the seventeenth century was produced in a period of immense spiritual and social change. The medieval craftsman, creatively independent and working within his own tradition, had by then been largely superseded as designer by the professional architect who interpreted the classical tradition, applied rules of proportion and selected types of ornamentation. Craftsmen who once had carved dragon, angel and cockatrice on beams and corner posts were now employed by wealthy patrons who wanted their houses to display opulent strapwork raised in diamonds, ovals and lozenges, adorned with their initials, date panels and motifs.

Pargeted designs

Much pargeting relies for its success upon understatement and simplicity. Timber-framed houses were constructed from posts and beams, the panels between them being filled with interwoven hazel rods and straw mixed with earth or clay. The structure of frames and associated window openings produced a simple rhythm encouraging a sympathetic surface decoration that celebrated regularity and order, uncompromised by modern features such as downpipes and flues. It took account of the spaces between and below windows, above doors, in dormers and gables, to achieve overall balance. Scattering pargeted elements all over the façade or grouping them irregularly was never a traditional approach, though that is not necessarily to dismiss it. But the design needed an appropriate visual strength, as it was to be viewed from a distance. Confidence was essential, but so was the sensitivity of application: a deep impression or profile might appear heavy or clumsy, especially when it was exact and repetitive; one that was too shallow or fine might disappear in certain light, although such delicacy could be an attraction. The same is true of borders; pargeting is like low-relief sculpture, responding to light and weathering. New designs need to be thought out before application starts, either drawn full-size on the building or plotted accurately on architect's drawings. There is no reason why the pargeter's repertoire cannot continually be extended to generate new patterns to suit new buildings.

The majority of pre-nineteenth-century pargeting occurs on buildings whose external walls comprise substantial timber frames that were hidden when the building was plastered over for draught-proofing and enhancement. Yet, perhaps because of the craftsman's familiarity with the timber-frame construction, much simple pargeting reflects the proportions of the timber-frame bays by means of single-line scratched or moulded borders demarcating blank panels, either square or rectangular. This arrangement may also have reduced the risks of the plaster cracking by allowing stresses to be dispersed through the lines of incised patterns.

A traditional elaboration was to fill the blank panels with decorative patterns so

Details of High Victorian pargeting designs from the excellent range at Radwinter, Essex. These particularly decorative patterns are from the almshouses.

9

Above: *A simple but very effective incised diagonal pattern on a house in Yoxford, Suffolk.*

Right: *A form of pargeting in which individual motifs are impressed into the centres of panels.*

Above: *Detail of impressed decoration at Clare, Suffolk.*

Right: *Some of the tools used for pargeting, including a seven-toothed comb, a profile mould for 'running' borders, a stamp for impressing fantails and a device for making a basket-weave pattern.*

that the whole façade of a building became a grid of smooth plaster separating decorated panels. There were many ways of elaborating the effect, and the most complex pargeting builds up three-dimensional decoration with friezes, swags and life-sized figures.

Decorative patterns can be incised, pricked or scratched into the plaster surface, and 'combed work' or 'stick work' is produced with combs made of wood with five, six or seven teeth. Old saw blades, large forks or nails are also used, and a pointed stick or group of sticks tied together can be used to make a fan pattern. The simple design known as 'sparrow picking' requires a triangular tool with three teeth. Effective patterns produced in easily flowing arrangements with these basic tools include bird's feet, chevrons, lattices, ropes, herringbones, the guilloche pattern, scales, cable, scallops and fantails. They may extend all over the wall without any discernible borders, and lack of precision contributes greatly to their overall success: a delight of older pargeting is its sublimation of individual strokes to achievement of overall effect.

10

Above, from left to right: *Detail of impressed trefoil and star decorations at Coggeshall, Essex. Detail of a raised round and square pattern, greatly restored, at Lavenham, Suffolk. 'Interchanging squares'.*

Above: *Detail of 'interchanging squares' and fantails. This example is particularly precise and uniform.*

Above: *Four different surface textures around a dummy window at Braintree, Essex.*

Right: *Templates for stamping patterns into wet plaster and moulds for 'running' borders, laid on a plasterer's hawk.*

Indented, imprinted or stamped designs can be produced by pressing into the wet plaster surface simple templates and by using rollers of wood or metal. A favourite motif is 'interchanging squares', combining short vertical and horizontal lines; circles are also popular, together with basket-weave squares and impressed dots. Stamps are best hand-made to avoid undue harshness: they can be carved from a clean white softwood such as sycamore. When not in use, the stamping tool should be kept in a bucket of sawdust to control its moisture content. Gentle lack of uniformity, like personal handwriting, may be desirable in the result, especially in

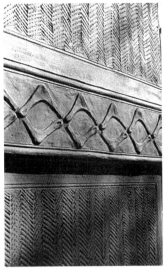

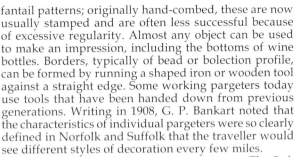

fantail patterns; originally hand-combed, these are now usually stamped and are often less successful because of excessive regularity. Almost any object can be used to make an impression, including the bottoms of wine bottles. Borders, typically of bead or bolection profile, can be formed by running a shaped iron or wooden tool against a straight edge. Some working pargeters today use tools that have been handed down from previous generations. Writing in 1908, G. P. Bankart noted that the characteristics of individual pargeters were so clearly defined in Norfolk and Suffolk that the traveller would see different styles of decoration every few miles.

There may be symbolism in some patterns. The Suffolk cable or rope pattern may have been linked to the hemp industry, and the fleur-de-lis, mitre and rowell (spur-wheel) patterns in Lavenham, Suffolk, relate to the cloth industry that flourished there. The cornucopia signified plenty, the dolphin affection, the vine eternal love or friendship.

The sharpness and definition of older patterns may have been reduced by the build-up of successive coats of limewash used for protection and decoration.

Above: *Rich surface texture with a 'boomerang' frieze.*

Below: *Detail of rope patterning.*

Above: *Detail of fantail decoration.*

Left: *Arms and crests above a vine frieze at Hadleigh, Suffolk.*

Below left: *Detail of combed basket-weave surface decoration.*

Below right: *Swirling foliage decoration at Hadleigh, Suffolk.*

Unusual motifs in a frieze at Lavenham, Suffolk.

More complicated patterns may project proud of the façade, and heavy features were restrained structurally with spikes or sometimes built up with broken brick or tiles. Moulds of wood or beeswax were employed to make plaques that could be embedded in the wall plaster, as well as sets of initials, date stones, garlands, oval bands or single motifs such as Tudor roses, sun heads, crowns, rampant lions, eagles or flowers. These ornaments could be used together in decorative friezes – popular at the level of the first floor, where the additional weight could easily be tied back –

Far left: *Detail of a frieze typical in Yoxford, Suffolk. The irregular impressed dotted panels above and below it would have been formed with a tool like that shown on page 11.*

Left: *A frieze terminating in a sea monster at Yoxford, Suffolk.*

such as the sea-monster frieze used on several occasions in Yoxford, Suffolk. From there it was only a short step to the elaborations of trailing vines, hops, honeysuckle and tendrils and the occasional decorative figure such as that nestling under eaves beside the great chimney at Colneford House, Essex. On the frontage of that house, large pargeted panels dated 1685 suggest tapestries hung between the first-floor windows.

Left and below: *Colneford House, Earls Colne, Essex. Fine swirling patterns beside the chimney (left), including a figure just below the eaves, contrast with more formal pargeting on the main façade. The imposing frontage features crisply pargeted panels, one dated 1685, hung like tapestries between the first-floor windows.*

Very ornate strapwork patterns survive on one pargeted first-floor wall of Garrison House, East Street, Wivenhoe, Essex.

Yet more complex are the all-over floral patterns and elaborate geometrical strapwork raised proud of the building façade. They evoke the powers and energies of the natural world in buildings such as Garrison House, Wivenhoe, Essex. Patterns could also be generated in reverse by placing templates of thin wood on the surface of the penultimate coat of plaster and plastering up to them: on removal of the template a pattern would emerge. There is a good example of this technique at Coddenham, Suffolk.

Finally, there is older pargeting that is as much sculpture as surface relief, and this ranges from simple linework to elaborate figures, animals and birds. Much of that modelling is free-hand, raised by an expert using fingers and small tools. The examples remaining are few and probably not in their original form, yet they are tremendous, imbued with splendidly primitive qualities that most people see as spirited and vigorous. There is a fine example at the former Sun Inn, Saffron Walden, Essex, where a good collection of birds and beasts – including the burlesque and grotesque – rise up above fine and varied plaster textures, culminating in two large figures dominating a gable. Nobody knows what they represent, though legend has it that one of them is Thomas Hickathrift, a local carter, who freed the people of Wisbech by killing a marauding giant with the axle of his cart. Perhaps the story was brought here by carters who once lodged in the inn. More sophisticated but generally shallower reliefs were produced on civic buildings in the period around 1920.

Strong simple patterning, unusually at ground-floor level, on a pair of cottages at Stutton, Suffolk. Crowe Hall, immediately adjacent, includes decorated seventeenth-century ceilings: there may well be a link.

The former Sun Inn at Saffron Walden, Essex, displays a wide variety of pargeted subject matter. In common with many other examples of elaborate pargeting, there is a shortage of documentation about the origin of the wide variety of decorative motifs.

15

Left, from top to bottom: *Simple linework and roundels on the street frontage of Nethergate House, Clare, Suffolk. Swag decoration with the date 1693 at Hadleigh, Suffolk. Patterns generated within the thickness of the plaster surface at Coddenham, Suffolk.*

After the years of austere Puritan rule from 1649 to 1660, Charles II returned to England, bringing with him a range of foreign affectations and continental fashions, including exuberant decoration. Pargeters joined the national mood with compositions gathering together scrolls, swags, cornucopias of fruit and flowers, dolphins, vases, coats of arms, date panels, pilasters, cruciform shapes and subjects projected upon cartouches. These related well to the carved arcading and foliated strapwork of contemporary English furniture, and such ornamentation was a development of an earlier intricacy of carved beams, bargeboards and bressumers.

Archive drawings, engravings and old photographs of buildings believed to date from this period show how elaborate such decoration could be. A view of Little Moor Fields, London, indicates great flower-encrusted storey-high scrolls each side of a bay window; in London Wall, plaster cherubs and young women are surrounded with flowers. In Canterbury bacchanalian putti disport themselves amongst the tendrils of vines. An old print of Old Fishpond Houses, London, indicates dolphins, sea monsters, a storey-high Venus emerging from her shell and a variety of aquatic themes including fish hooked and hanging and fish beached.

Amongst the best-known surviving examples of pargeting from the Restoration period is the Ancient House in the Buttermarket, Ipswich, also called Robert Sparrowe's House after the widely travelled spice merchant and grocer who commissioned its exuberant pargeting in the 1660s. The upper storeys carry heavily moulded swags of fruit and leaves, birds, flowers, even garlands of fish and instruments, together with the gilded coat of arms of Charles II, who visited Ipswich in 1668. Here Neptune with a trident rides a

16

Old Fishpond Houses, London from 'A History of Renaissance Architecture in England', by Sir Reginald Blomfield.

seahorse; there is a Pelican in her Piety, and a shepherd and shepherdess (together representing Water, Air and Earth). Atlas supports the globe; St George vanquishes the dragon, and the main panels below the oriel windows are resplendent with figures, buildings and animals, each panel representing one of the four known continents. Within the courtyard a chariot is drawn by plumed horses in a composition that Claire Gapper notes has been identified by Anthony Wells-Cole as a copy of an engraving depicting 'The Task of Worldly Power' from *The Divine Charge to the Three Estates* published *c*.1585. It is not

Above left: *Little Moor Fields, London, from 'Antient Topography of London', by J. T. Smith. Smith linked 'foliated' decoration to the visit of Henrietta Maria to London, encouraging interest in the popular French scrollwork and foliage designs of John le Pautre and Stefano Della Bella.*

Above right: *A house on the south side of London Wall drawn in 1808 by J. T. Smith, attributed to the time of Charles I but no longer fashionable (in fact the gingerbread maker in the house on the left stripped his frontage in the 1760s).*

The pargeting on the Ancient House, Ipswich, Suffolk, is amongst the most outstanding in England.

clear how that relates to the putative Zacchaeus in the tree.

As with any fashion, pargeting fell out of favour. In 1663 Sir Balthazar Gerbier foreshadowed a move away from excess in his *Counsel and Advice to All Builders*, urging 'moderation in the ordering of ornaments'. Under 'ridiculous ornaments', he particularly recommended the shunning of 'incongruities, as many (pretending knowledge in Ornaments) have committed, by placing between windows Pilasters, through whose bodies Lions are represented to creep without any necessity'. In 1760 Horace Walpole described the decoration at Hardwick Hall as a 'monstrous frieze in miserable plaster relief'. By 1810 J. T. Smith, in a book full of drawings, could only mock 'one of the few remaining foliated fronts in London' from the time of Charles I, when 'it was much in fashion ... to decorate the fronts of houses with compositions in plaister of the most ridiculous subjects', such as 'shepherds, shepherdesses, sheep etc nearly the size of life' – citing the Ancient House at Ipswich.

18

The pargeting carried out in the eighteenth century and much of the nineteenth was rarely on buildings of consequence. It seems to have been generally restricted to the surface decoration of vernacular buildings, including cottages, farmhouses and rectories, having the status of a rural craft rather like thatching.

In the last decades of the nineteenth century a group of architects looked back to and were inspired by the 'Arts and Crafts' skills of an earlier age. One of their leaders was Norman Shaw, who in 1871-3 built New Zealand Chambers, Leadenhall Street, London (no longer standing). Mark Girouard (*Sweetness and Light*, Clarendon Press, 1977) described it thus: 'pargeting of splendidly lush quality was applied below the windows and on the immense coved cornice which crowned the façade' (illustrated in *Building News*, 5th September 1873). He linked its conception directly to the Ancient House at Ipswich. At about the same time Norman Shaw's partner Eden Nesfield got the opportunity to continue the theme in Essex when the centre of the thatched village of Radwinter was destroyed by fire in 1874. It was rebuilt over

some twenty years with new, pargeted walls, ranging from the church porch to the Reading Room and Dispensary and pargeted shops, cottages and almshouses. All were executed in a highly decorated render with patterns ranging from the delicate to substantial, muscular swags and armorial panels – the whole ensemble providing an excellent display of the diversity and sophistication of High Victorian pargeting. An important

Above and right: A wide range of High Victorian pargeting designs can be seen in the rebuilding of the village of Radwinter, Essex, following a fire in 1874. One of the most impressive buildings is the Dispensary, where the baroque-inspired use of undecorated cementitious render has produced distinctive façades, crisply executed.

Left and below: *Beautifully executed pargeted designs incised into the upper walls and curved eaves of this little frontage in North Street, Sudbury, Suffolk, are combined with colourful mosaic decoration, dated 1876, evocative of that period.*

distinction between this and earlier pargeting was the addition of significant quantities of cement to the mix, the 1877 *Building News* recommending, for 'external plasterwork', one part of Portland cement to three parts of clean sharp sand; the implications of this are discussed below. Particularly decorative essays combined pargeting with mosaics and other surface finishes – there is a lovely small-scale example, dated 1876, in North Street, Sudbury, Suffolk.

High Victorian pargeting was often self-consciously designed rather than expressing a vernacular tradition, and thus more usually academically revivalist than instinctive. Thus it tended to exhibit precision, architectural control and consistency, whether in virtuoso displays of free, narrative 'Jacobethan' strapwork and figures in relief or in more controlled 'stamp-work', as in the subtle, beautifully crafted 1884 almshouses at Sible Hedingham, Essex, or the more ostentatious frontage in Abbeygate Street, Bury St Edmunds.

Left and above: *The almshouses dated 1884 at Sible Hedingham, Essex, are distinctively patterned with unusual impressed and zigzag decoration. The ease with which the complex design sits happily on the building is testimony to considerable skill.*

The geometric precision of the clearly defined panels of pargeting on this frontage in Abbeygate Street, Bury St Edmunds, Suffolk, is typical of later nineteenth-century work in harder plasters and renders.

The interest in pargeting expressed by Shaw's office had developed significantly by 1894 when a design for a country house by Gerald Horsley (1862–1917) was featured in *Builder* magazine (3rd February 1894). It included large first-floor relief panels depicting pastoral Pre-Raphaelite scenes, appropriate imagery from a founder of the Art Workers' Guild, yet it was probably never executed. Arguably, that work was closer in spirit to the elaborate European stucco decoration exemplified at the 1902 Turin Exhibition of Modern Decorative Art than ever it was to the tradition of English pargeting, a seam of which emerged in suburban development. A great number of middle-class English houses built in the period 1870-1914 were remarkable in their heterogeneity of style. They expressed all sorts of techniques and materials, many being revivalist – Italianate, Gothic with mullioned windows, Dutch gables, round windows. Inevitably there was also some pargeting, expressed in flowery gables and friezes cut into panels above window openings combined with splayed and bracketed cornices. In sheltered streets like those round

Decoration of floral designs pressed into the render of this nineteenth-century frontage in Saffron Walden, Essex.

Left and below: *Pargeted patterns, raised and incised, in the gables and eaves of houses around Muswell Hill, London.*

Muswell Hill, London, behind little hedges of privet or *Lonicera nitida*, house after house has its red brick frontage and gable given additional swirling individuality by its very own panel of pargeting.

The revival of interest in pargeted designs continued into the twentieth century, most enthusiastically on houses in small towns and villages in Essex like Thaxted and Finchingfield, where the tradition of pargeting may never have completely faded. At the same time experiments took place with other sorts of surface decoration using assorted plasters and renders. For example, there was raised lettering such as the 'Fear God GR Honour the King' sign in Great Yeldham, Suffolk.

The few outstanding examples of pargeting from this period include some highly decorated civic buildings. One of the more dramatic examples, dating from 1910, fronts Cornhill, Bury St Edmunds. Jacobethan strapwork relief with caryatid decoration is punctuated by niches occupied by life-size figures such as St Edmund, above which a central pediment displays characters including what appears to be a medieval monarch. This sort of work was opulent yet expensive and sufficiently rare between the wars that in 1927 *Country Life*'s book on plasterwork declared that 'pargetry has gone out of fashion' (bad rough-cast being 'the order of the day'). But there remained some skills: when Croydon's, a jeweller's shop in Tavern Street, Ipswich, was rebuilt in 1931 it used pargeted devices to evoke the feeling of a much older building, as does the 'Elizabethan' relief on the building next door.

Today, there is a localised craft tradition of pargeting kept alive by a few individuals. Some

An elaborately decorated frontage at 15 Cornhill, Bury St Edmunds, Suffolk, 1910, by Michael Vyne Treleavan for Sir Joseph Boot.

22

Patterns are built up slowly with a variety of tools. This practical demonstration of pargeting with lime plaster was arranged by Essex County Council at Cressing Temple in 1998 to promote the technique.

modern pargeting has a very mechanical feel to it, and some well-meaning attempts to recreate designs have not been successful. Over-enthusiasm, particularly in the refurbishment of older buildings, can engender results that apparently try to show off every style of pargeting at once and to cover all available wall surfaces with it, blighting otherwise quite unassuming buildings, confusing proportion, hierarchy, order and even the historical development of the building. More enlightened practitioners who understand their material are bringing new thoughts and approaches to traditional techniques, producing their own interpretation of pargeting. The results vary, whether cut into hard cement renders or built up in softer materials, often depicting rural scenes, trees, wildlife, game and decorative patterns based on fruit and flowers. Some may appear naïve and unsophisticated, some over-sentimental; some are genuinely good. They can be found on back-street cottages, rural pubs and expensive new houses, and what they have in common is their desire to make personal a particular building.

In recent years the builders of housing estates have sometimes used a sort of pargeted decoration to try to blend new developments in with traditional stock. One surface texture in current use is produced by brushing the newly rendered surface with a stiff bristle brush, then ironing on a border against a blank surround. Simple, standardised friezes are deployed for similar reasons. Such approaches are rarely individual or craft-driven, and they tend to lack identity.

The façade of Croydon's shop in Tavern Street, Ipswich, Suffolk. It dates only from 1931, but the built-up plaster decoration is intended to give the appearance of a much earlier building.

Bankart's book 'The Art of the Plasterer', published in 1908, maintained that York was particularly rich in pargeted houses, citing these old prints of examples in Coney Street from the time of Charles I.

The purpose and techniques of the craft

As has been mentioned, the panels between the posts and beams of old timber-framed houses were filled with interwoven hazel rods, straw and earth or clay. A finishing coat of plaster or an earth daub provided a smooth, draught-proof, weather-resistant surface finished with limewash. Wattle and daub panels can be resilient, but they have often been replaced with soft red brick nogging, and ultimately many such buildings were rebuilt entirely in brickwork. Any plaster decoration on them would have been lost whenever rebuilding took place.

If the timber frame was well executed it might be exposed externally and limewashed along with the panels. Alternatively the plaster finish, often supported on timber laths, could be extended over the frame. When timber prices rose in the later sixteenth century this technique allowed the use of irregular and second-hand timbers within new construction and also enabled additions and structural modifications to be disguised, such as refronting a property and inserting upper floors or blocking up windows following window taxes. Thus Queen Elizabeth's Guest House, Canterbury, is a medieval house modernised and pargeted in the seventeenth century. Pargeting was a good way to give an old building a new lease of life.

Wooden laths, usually 25 mm wide and at least 1.2 metres long, hand-split along the grain, were cut from oak or beech and later from straight-grained red Baltic fir. Lengths were applied horizontally at a maximum 12.5 mm apart. They were flexible enough to accommodate some movement in the main frame whilst binding it together and retaining a degree of movement. Traditional plasters are not strictly waterproof and allow old buildings to breathe so that rain-driven moisture can

A modern pargeted frieze on the front of the Bell Inn, Bramfield, Suffolk, appropriately takes as its subject matter the production of beer.

evaporate from them (like a thick coat), unlike modern buildings, which tend to rely on keeping rainwater out by means of a weatherproof skin (like an unlined anorak). Traditional lime plasters also have an inherent degree of flexibility and allow limited movement, any minor cracking being filled with further coats of limewash; applying a proprietary waterproofing solution to such a surface is likely to lead to future problems.

Sand and lime are the basic constituents of plaster, mixed with the minimal amount of water necessary for workability. Some say that the sand should be sharp, clean and free from organic matter and salt (for example, 'river sand'), but earth is also used to encourage plasticity. Lime should be mature lime putty, but this can vary, depending upon its origin and hydraulic qualities. The purpose of the lime is to bind gently and allow the resulting coating to breathe, but it must be fully slaked or the surface finish may suffer, and sometimes non-hydraulic limes may be gauged with small quantities of cement to develop early strength. A mix that sets too quickly may not allow sufficient time for the pargeter to do his work; a mix that sets very slowly may risk being caught by frost. Traditional pargeting thus tended to be seasonal work, impossible to carry out all the year round, limited by freezing in the winter and excessive dryness in the summer (which could be modified by covering finished work with wet hessian). The orientation of the building may also have been significant, those facing due south evidently being less suitable for pargeting. Spring and autumn might have presented the best opportunities for slow and even drying, so in days past a pargeter might have been a local craftsman who could at other times of the year turn his hand to brickwork, tiling and flintwork.

It was recommended that the plaster should stand well before application of the first or 'backing' coat of 'coarse stuff', to even out the greatest irregularities. This first coat might be a mix of one measure of matured lime putty to three of sharp sand, plus a binder. Finely chopped hay, reeds or rye straw were used as a binder in cheaper work; in better-class work it was preferable to use animal hair, suitably washed. Horsehair was popular, as were short lengths of soft and rough cow or bullock hair, which grew longer when the animals were wintered in the open; it was

25

A new house with pargeted decoration near Long Melford, Suffolk. Its modern form and fenestration have required the adaptation of traditional pargeting techniques to produce an individual design.

scraped from the hides as a by-product of the leather industry that flourished in East Anglia when pargeting was at its height. One source recommended that the hair be well teased and that one pound (0.45 kg) of hair be used per 3 cubic feet (0.08 cubic metres) of the mix. In the later nineteenth century sawdust sometimes replaced hair as the binder. Additional ingredients recommended over the years included stable urine, road scrapings or stone grit, soot, wood scrapings, cheese, tallow (clarified animal or horse fat) and cow dung; some of these may have imparted useful characteristics not at present fully understood. They produced a viscous mix with the workability necessary for the pargeter to produce complex patterning.

The second or 'floating' coat might be proportioned three parts of lime putty to five parts of sharp sand (never stronger than the backing coat), usually omitting the binder. It was applied before the first coat was completely dry. Pre-cast plaster decorations could be incorporated into the composition as it was executed. The application of a third coat tended to be restricted to more exposed locations. Such mixes, where thick, could take months to dry (rather than go hard) and would eventually be decorated in limewash, naturally off-white or possibly tinted with a naturally fading earth colour such as apple green, ochre yellow or earthy red. One commentator suggested finishing with linseed oil.

A modern relief panel on a building in Suffolk shows typical rural life in the surrounding countryside.

26

Far left: *Modern relief decoration on tea rooms in Finchingfield, Essex.*

Left: *Unusual floral decoration in high relief using a cement render in Clare, Suffolk.*

Right and far right: *Formal and free-form decoration using a cement render in Braintree, Essex.*

Pargeting is not restricted to timber-framed buildings. In the later nineteenth century, when there was a revival of the craft, and later, the technique was applied to brick buildings. It is now recognised that these present a less flexible, more regular and precise setting, where careful consideration needs to be given to such matters as suction, thermal movement and cement content.

From the later nineteenth century there was increased use of Portland cement in construction. The benefits were seen to be an earlier development of greater strength in mortar and render, thereby speeding construction and the development of water-proof finishes. In time it became clear that there were disadvantages too, such as brittleness and inflexibility, giving an increased tendency to crack and allow water to penetrate. A coating with a high cement content demanded that the craftsman worked quickly before it set. Modern fine-grained cement renders risk producing pargeting with hard edges, a lack of subtlety and a mechanical appearance. Never-theless most revivalist pargeting since the later nineteenth century has been carried out in harder mortars.

High Street, Maidstone, Kent. A drawing by W. Bliss Saunders from Bankart's 'The Art of the Plasterer' of a building no longer in existence. Decorative panels – filling storey-height bays between the upper windows – are pargeted with swags, flowers, fruit, animals and foliage around a variety of figures.

Contemplating repairs

Anybody trying to repair decayed pargeting should seek expert assistance. The plaster can fail for several reasons. Years of application of limewash may have built up excessive thickness, blurring the pattern and encouraging the plaster to fracture: it may be possible to remove this by laborious flaking with a scalpel or an air abrasive pencil (for experienced conservators only!). Unsuitable finishes or repairs may have trapped moisture in the plaster, causing it or the backing to decay; alternatively, small cracks may have opened up, allowing water to get behind the plaster face but not evaporate through it, causing the plaster to lose its key. There may have been structural movement in the main frame too, but an historic timber frame can be consolidated without stripping off pargeting. If the plaster is bulging dangerously there may be philosophical as well as practical considerations: whether to attempt to tie back, salvage pieces or to strip and start again.

Before commencing repair, record photographs, dimensioned drawings and squeeze moulds should be taken and archives consulted. Documents may clarify whether what exists is original or faithful to the original pattern, and the local planning authority will confirm whether the building is listed or in a Conservation Area, in which case a formal application may be required before work commences.

One of the difficulties in dating pargeting is the way in which it may have been renewed in part or in whole. In the post-war period it has not been uncommon to strip off pargeted decorations and then scatter them, like trophies, across a rebuilt façade in the name of 'restoration'. When the Ancient House in Clare was 'restored' after the Second World War it is said that the workmen had no drawings to work

Recent pargeting using many different patterns, including animal shapes, at Bean's Cottages near Clare, Suffolk.

Detail of restoration at Swan Street, Boxford, Suffolk, where the ornamental frieze is titled 'XVII Century'. For the avoidance of doubt, '1975' is added below.

A combination of pargeting and painted decoration can be seen on this house in Benhall, Suffolk.

29

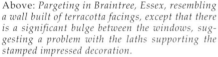

Above: *Pargeting in Braintree, Essex, resembling a wall built of terracotta facings, except that there is a significant bulge between the windows, suggesting a problem with the laths supporting the stamped impressed decoration.*

Right: *Old pargeting in Bradford Street, Braintree, Essex, which has been almost obscured by a build-up of successive layers of limewash.*

from or moulds to refer to, and they stripped away much of the existing plaster before renewing it. But what they removed was not original, since it did not include the fabulous winged monster that was once displayed below one of the windows. So the result is only a rather approximate copy of a copy. Other buildings have doubtless been approached in a similar way.

If pargeting is beyond repair and all the plaster is removed from a structural frame that is to be retained, what should replace it? Some might say that historic pargeting, once lost, cannot be replaced, and that therefore it should be renewed in plain plaster. Others might seek the restoration of the original design, plus a date stone for reference. A third way would be to make a new pargeted façade that in its patterns and layout would reflect something of the character of the people who commissioned it and of those who crafted it. The latter option encourages development of craft skills, understanding of techniques and materials and a pride in artistic integrity and needs to be commissioned by an employer with vision. He might also apply it to a completely new building.

One of the fascinations of English architecture is the way in which ideas are reinterpreted over and over again as style, materials and other influences interact, often quite unexpectedly. It would be a mistake to say that there will be no further innovations in pargeting.

Further reading

Ashurst, John. *Mortars, Plaster and Renders in Conservation.* Gower, 1988.
Bankart, G.P. *The Art of the Plasterer.* Batsford, 1908.
Batsford, Harry, and Fry, Charles. *The English Cottage.* Batsford, 1938.
Beard, Geoffrey. *Decorative Plasterwork in Great Britain.* Phaidon, 1975.
Beard, Geoffrey. *National Trust Book of The English House Interior.* Viking, 1990.
Besant, Sir Walter. *London in the Time of the Tudors.* Adam & Charles Black, 1904.
Blomfield, Reginald. *A History of Renaissance Architecture in England 1500–1800* (volumes 1 and 2). George Bell, 1897.
Brown, R.J. *English Farmhouses.* Robert Hale, 1982.
Brown, R.J. *The English Country Cottage.* Robert Hale, 1990.
Chesterton, M. *Suffolk Building.* East Suffolk County Council, 1949.
Davey, Peter. *Arts and Crafts Architecture.* Phaidon, 1995.
Essex County Council. *Traditional Building Materials in Essex: Pargeting.* 1982.
Gapper, Claire. *Plasterers and Plasterwork in City, Court and Country, c.1530–c.1640.* Unpublished PhD thesis, University of London, 1998.
Gerbier, Sir Balthazar. *Counsel and Advice to All Builders.* 1663.
Girouard, Mark. *Sweetness and Light.* Clarendon Press, 1977.
Gloag, John. *Early English Decorative Detail.* Alec Tiranti, 1965.
Jourdain, M. *English Decorative Plasterwork of the Renaissance.* Batsford, 1926.
Jones, Sydney R. *The Village Homes of England.* Bracken Books, 1912.
Lloyd, David W. *Historic Towns of East Anglia.* Victor Gollancz, 1989.
Long, Helen. *The Edwardian House.* Manchester University Press, 1993.
Messent, C.J.W. 'The Old Cottages and Farmhouses of Suffolk', *Proceedings of Suffolk Institute of Archaeology*, 1934-6, volume 22, pages 244-63.
Millar, William. *Plastering Plain and Decorative.* 1897; reprinted Donhead, 1998.
Moxon, Joseph. *Mechanick Exercises.* 1678.
Muthesius, Stefan. *The English Terraced House.* Yale University Press, 1982.
Oliver, Basil. *Old Houses and Village Buildings in East Anglia.* Batsford, 1912.
Penoyre, John and Jane. *Decorative Plasterwork in the Houses of Somerset 1500–1700.* Somerset County Council, 1994.
Quiney, Anthony. *English Domestic Architecture: Kent Houses.* Antique Collectors' Club, 1993.
Reid, Richard. *The Shell Book of Cottages.* Michael Joseph, 1977.
Salzman, L.F. *Building in England down to 1540.* Oxford University Press, 1952.
Sandon, Eric. *Suffolk Houses – a Study of Domestic Architecture.* Antique Collectors' Club, 1977.
Schofield, John. *Medieval London Houses.* Yale University Press, 1994.
Smith, J.T. *Antient Topography of London.* c.1792.
Turner, Laurence. *Decorative Plasterwork in Great Britain.* Country Life, 1927.
Wells-Cole, Anthony. *Art and Decoration in Elizabethan and Jacobean England.* Yale University Press, 1997.

SOME SOURCE BOOKS FOR PARGETED DESIGNS
Blume, Hans. *Quinque Columnarum.* Zurich, 1550.
Dietterlin, Wendel. *Architectura.* Nuremburg, late sixteenth century.
Peacham, Henry. *Minerva Britanna or; A Garden of Heroical Deuises furnish'd and adorned with Emblems and Impresas.* 1612.
Platt, Sir Hugh. *The Jewel House of Art and Nature.* 1594.
Quarles, Francis. *Emblems, Divine and Moral.* 1635.
Recorde, Richard. *Castle of Knowledge.* 1561.
Shute, John. *The First and Chief Groundes of Architecture.* 1563.
Vries, J. Vredeman de. *Architectura.* Antwerp, 1563.
Vries, J. Vredeman de. *Compartimentia.* Antwerp, 1566.
Wither, George. *Emblems, Ancient and Modern.* 1635.

Places to visit

There is only a comparatively small number of easily accessible buildings which exhibit dramatic pargeting; on the other hand many towns and villages contain streets or clusters of buildings ,where there is group value in collections of diverse but perhaps less spectacular examples. The following list thus includes specific buildings, streets and villages where there may be several examples of pargeting.

ESSEX
Braintree: Bradford Street.
Dedham: High Street.
Earls Colne: Colneford House.
Newport: Crown House.
Radwinter: most of the buildings around the church.
Saffron Walden: the former Sun Inn.
Wivenhoe: Garrison House.
The villages of Cooksmill Green, Coggeshall, Finchingfield, Great Waltham, Sible Hedingham, and Thaxted.

HERTFORDSHIRE
Hertford: High Street and Fore Street.
St Albans: Fishpool Street.
The villages of Braughing, Little Hadham.

KENT
Canterbury: Queen Elizabeth Guest House, High Street.

Faversham: West Street.
Loose: Wool House.
Maidstone: Bank Street.

NORFOLK
East Dereham: Bishop Bonner's Cottages.

SUFFOLK
Bury St Edmunds: Cornhill, Abbeygate Street, Whiting Street.
Clare: Ancient House.
Hadleigh: High Street and Benton Street.
Ipswich: Ancient House, Tavern Street, The Buttermarket.
Lavenham: High Street, Church Street, Water Street.
The villages of Benhall, Boxford, Bramfield, Brandeston, Cavendish, Great Yeldham, Stutton, Yoxford.

Details of pargeted decoration on the front of the Ancient House, Ipswich, Suffolk, dating from the 1660s.

32